U.S. HISTORY IN REVIEW

The Industrial Revolution

BY KATHRYN WALTON

Enslow PUBLISHING

Please visit our website, www.enslow.com. For a free color catalog of all our high-quality books, call toll free 1-800-398-2504 or fax 1-877-980-4454.

Library of Congress Cataloging-in-Publication Data
Names: Walton, Kathryn, 1993- author.
Title: The industrial revolution / Kathryn Walton.
Description: Buffalo, New York : Enslow Publishing, [2024] | Series: U.S. history in review | Includes index.
Identifiers: LCCN 2023003423 (print) | LCCN 2023003424 (ebook) | ISBN 9781978536180 (library binding) | ISBN 9781978536173 (paperback) | ISBN 9781978536197 (ebook)
Subjects: LCSH: Industrial revolution–Juvenile literature. | CYAC: Social change–United States–Juvenile literature.
Classification: LCC HC103 .W345 2024 (print) | LCC HC103 (ebook) | DDC 338.0973–dc23/eng/20230126
LC record available at https://lccn.loc.gov/2023003423
LC ebook record available at https://lccn.loc.gov/2023003424

Published in 2024 by
Enslow Publishing
2544 Clinton Street
Buffalo, NY 14224

Portions of this work were originally authored by Seth Lynch and published as *The Industrial Revolution*. All new material in this edition authored by Kathryn Walton.

Designer: Leslie Taylor
Editor: Natalie Humphrey

Photo credits: Cover Everett Collection/Shutterstock.com; series art (grunge flag) Andrey Kuzmin/Shutterstock.com; series art (stamp icon) Stocker_team/Shutterstock.com; series art (font) santstock/Shutterstock.com; p. 5 Dusan Pavlic/Shutterstock.com; p. 7 (background) EWY Media/Shutterstock.com, (inset) Name des Zeichners nicht lesbar./ https://commons.wikimedia.org/wiki/File:Zeichnung_Spinning_jenny.jpg; p. 8 chrisdorney/Shutterstock.com; p. 9 stock-images/Shutterstock.com; p. 11 (mill) Eifel Kreutz/istockphoto.com, (Slater) National Biographical Publishing Company/ https://commons.wikimedia.org/wiki/File:Samuel_Slater_industrialist.jpg; p. 13 (using cotton gin) Everett Collection/Shutterstock.com, (inset) Tom Murphy VII/ https://commons.wikimedia.org/wiki/File:Cotton_gin_EWM_2007.jpg; p. 15 Flint, Charles L. (Charles Louis)/ https://commons.wikimedia.org/wiki/File:The American farmer. A complete agricultural library, with useful facts for the household, devoted to farming in all its departments and details (1882) (14741203956).jpg; p. 17 (top) MaxyM/Shutterstock.com, (bottom) leonavt/Shutterstock.com; p. 19 Everett Collection/Shutterstock.com; p. 20 Florida Memory/Flickr.com; p. 21 Everett Collection/Shutterstock.com; p. 23 Everett Collection/Shutterstock.com; p. 25 Everett Collection/Shutterstock.com; p. 26 Everett Collection/Shutterstock.com; p. 27 (light bulbs) Victority/Shutterstock.com, (Edison) Everett Collection/Shutterstock.com; p. 29 jamesteohart/Shutterstock.com.

Printed in the United States of America

CPSIA compliance information: Batch #CSENS24: For further information, contact Enslow Publishing at 1-800-398-2504.

Contents

Words in the glossary appear in ***bold*** *the first time they are used in the text.*

What Is a Revolution?

A revolution is a big change in the way people live, work, or understand things. The Industrial Revolution was a period of **economic** change across the United States and the world. The economy would move from one based on agriculture to one based on industry.

Learn More

Industry is the system of making many goods with machinery, particularly in factories. Agriculture is the job of farming, including raising animals and growing food.

illustration of the Industrial Revolution

Great Britain Starts the Revolution

The Industrial Revolution started in Great Britain. It began in the mid-1700s with two machines: the spinning jenny and the **improved** steam **engine**. The spinning jenny is a machine that spins a lot of thread or yarn at the same time. This lets people make cloth faster.

Learn More

Great Britain didn't want to share these new **inventions**. The country knew it had an economic edge over other countries because of them.

the spinning jenny

Thomas Savery created an early steam engine in the late 1600s. But by the 1760s, James Watt had made it better. His improvements made the engine more efficient, or less wasteful. Steam engines would soon power the new trains, boats, and factories of the Industrial Revolution.

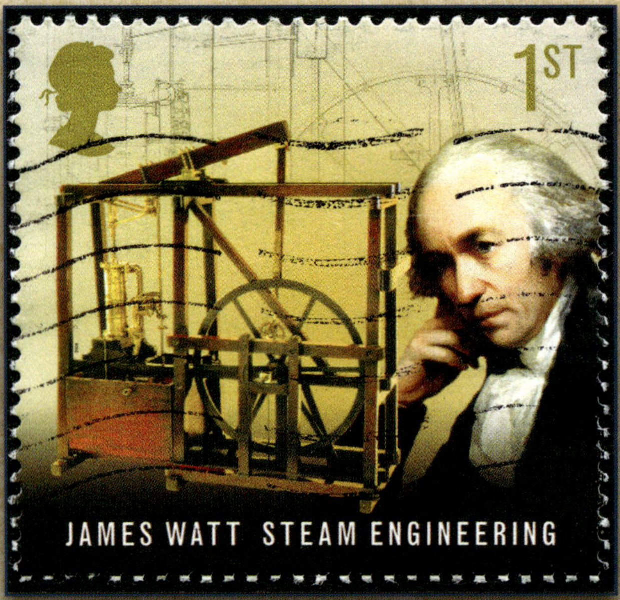

Learn More

British businessmen brought the Industrial Revolution to other countries, such as Belgium. The revolution would later spread around the world.

Samuel Slater

Samuel Slater is called the father of the American factory system. He brought the Industrial Revolution to the United States by **memorizing** plans for British textile machines. He built the first factory in the United States, a cotton mill, in 1790 in Rhode Island.

Samuel Slater

Learn More

A textile is a type of cloth that is knit or woven. Cotton mills are factories that turn cotton into textiles. Like many other factories at the time, Slater's cotton mill was powered by water.

The Cotton Gin

In 1794, Eli Whitney **patented** a machine called the cotton gin. It removed seeds from the cotton plant. Because the machine cleaned cotton faster, plantations, or large farms, could grow and sell more cotton. This made cotton an important crop for the southern economy.

cotton gin

Learn More

There was more work on plantations as the call for cotton grew. Because people had to pick cotton by hand, plantation owners bought more **enslaved** people to do this.

More Farming Tools

Plows and other machines also helped change farming in the United States. Between 1797 and the 1830s, people patented many kinds of plows. These and other machinery allowed farmers to produce more crops for less money. Many farmworkers lost their jobs to these new machines.

Learn More

People needed more natural **resources**, such as coal, to make and power some machinery. They opened new mines across the United States to get these resources. Some out-of-work farmers found jobs in these mines.

From Farm to Factory

Farmworkers who lost their jobs had to find different ways to make money. Many out-of-work farmworkers headed to cities to find new jobs in factories. Cities such as Boston, Massachusetts; Chicago, Illinois; and New York City grew because of this.

Learn More

Many factory jobs didn't need farmers to learn special skills. While this made work easier to find, the unskilled jobs were often boring. The work was also repetitive, or had the same action over and over again.

A Better Life in Cities

After the **Civil War**, cities grew even more. Around 25 million people from other countries moved to the United States between 1866 and 1915. Many came from Europe and settled in big cities. They saw the United States' new industries as a chance for work and a better life.

Learn More

With the amount of people coming to the United States, cities quickly became overcrowded. There weren't always good, safe places for people to live.

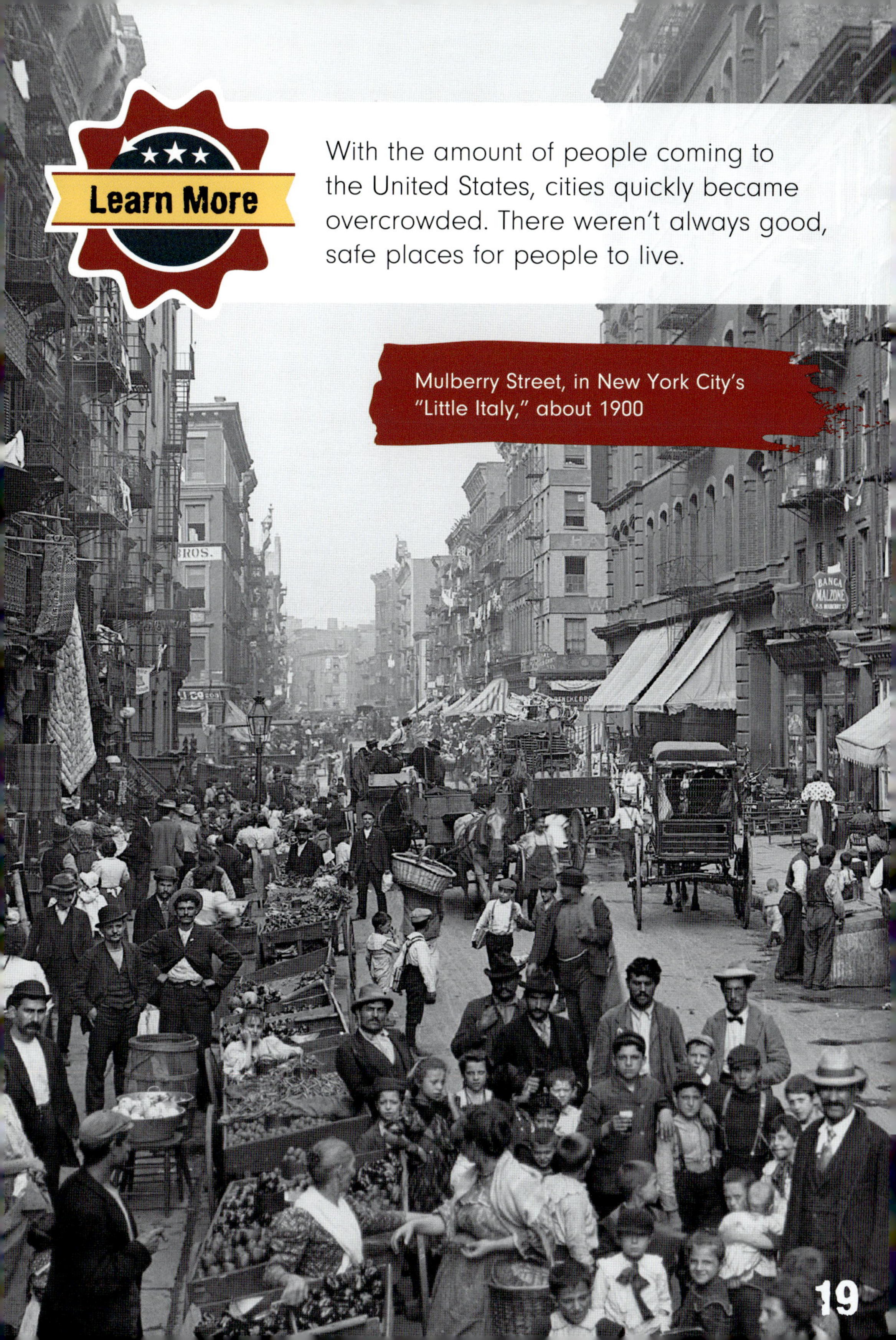

Mulberry Street, in New York City's "Little Italy," about 1900

Many freedmen, or people who used to be enslaved, moved to the North after the Civil War. They were treated somewhat better there and found jobs in northern factories. This also helped them get away from southerners who had fought to keep them enslaved.

Learn More

Other formerly enslaved people stayed in the South. Some became sharecroppers instead. Sharecroppers were people who rented land from plantation owners. In return, the owners took some of their crops.

Factory Conditions

Factory workers often worked in bad **conditions**. Factory workdays could be 10 to 12 hours long for little pay. Some of the work that people needed to do was unsafe. Children often worked in factories to earn money for their families.

Learn More

In the 1930s, the U.S. government made laws to protect working teenagers and stop children under 14 from working.

Industrial Improvements

The lives of U.S. **citizens** were changed by the Industrial Revolution. During this time, travel became much easier than it was before. Railroads crisscrossed the country, making it more possible to move people and goods from place to place.

steamboats on a Mississippi River dock, 1905

Learn More

Mass-produced goods, or those created in large numbers, started to take the place of homemade goods. Businesses used steamboats and trains to ship these items.

The Industrial Revolution didn't just change travel. It also changed **communication**. The first **telegram** was sent in 1844. Alexander Graham Bell patented the telephone on March 7, 1876. In 1915, Bell made the first cross-country phone call.

operator for the American Telephone and Telegraph Company, 1885

Learn More

Thomas Edison, among other scientists and inventors, helped make electricity part of everyday life during the Industrial Revolution. Electricity is a type of energy that usually flows through wires and can be used to power machines.

Changing the World

After the Industrial Revolution started, there was no way to stop it. In fact, many historians believe the Industrial Revolution doesn't have a true start or end date. Even today, people are creating more inventions to change our world!

Learn More

From the spinning jenny to the first cell phone, there has been no lack of inventions to improve our day-to-day lives!

Timeline

1712
The first successful modern steam engine is created.

1760s
The steam engine is improved by James Watt.

1770
The spinning jenny is patented.

1790
Samuel Slater opens his first factory.

1794
The cotton gin is patented by Eli Whitney.

1830s
Improved farming machines begin replacing workers.

1844
The first telegram is sent from Washington, D.C., to Baltimore, Maryland.

1861-1865
The American Civil War is fought.

1876
Alexander Graham Bell patents the telephone.

1869
A cross-country, or transcontinental, railroad is finished.

Glossary

citizen: Someone who lives in a country legally and has certain rights.

Civil War: A war fought from 1861 to 1865 in the United States between the Union (the Northern states) and the Confederacy (the Southern states).

communication: The act of using words to give and receive information.

condition: The state in which someone or something lives or works.

economic: Having to do with the money made in an area and how it is made.

engine: A machine that makes power.

enslaved: Having to do with being owned by another person and forced to work without pay.

improve: To make better.

memorize: To learn something so well that you are able to remember it perfectly.

patent: To have a piece of paper from the government that gives a person the rights to a design, machine, or process for a time.

plow: A farming device that is used to dig soil to prepare it for planning seeds.

resource: A usable supply of something.

telegram: A message that is sent by a telegraph machine using electricity and wires.

For More Information

Books

Harts, Shannon H. *Mark Twain and Nikola Tesla*. Buffalo, NY: Gareth Stevens Publishing, 2022.

Johnson, Jordan. *How the Steam Engine Changed the World*. Buffalo, NY: Cavendish Square Publishing, 2019.

Website

Kid Citizens

www.kidcitizen.net/episodes-blog/congress-and-child-labor

Learn more about what Congress did to end child labor after the Industrial Revolution.

Publisher's note to educators and parents: *Our editors have carefully reviewed this website to ensure that it is suitable for students. Many websites change frequently, however, and we cannot guarantee that a site's future contents will continue to meet our high standards of quality and educational value. Be advised that students should be closely supervised whenever they access the internet.*

Index